CONTENTS

AFGHANISTAN IS A LANDLOCKED COUNTRY IN CENTRAL ASIA, *bigger than France or most states in the USA. Much of the country is mountainous, with peaks in the Hindu Kush range rising up to 7,500 m (24,600 ft). Afghanistan's climate has the widest temperature range in the world, with summer highs of 53°C (127°F) and winter lows of −50°C (−58°F).*

THE COUNTRY

Kabul, the capital of Afghanistan, lies in the east of the country. The other major cities are Qandahar, Herat, Mazar-e-Sharif and Jalalabad. Most Afghans live in villages or small towns in the wild and remote countryside. Afghanistan borders Pakistan to its east and south, Iran to its west, Turkmenistan, Uzbekistan and Tajikistan to its north, and, at its very extreme eastern end, shares a very short mountainous frontier with China.

THE PEOPLE

The exact number of people living in Afghanistan is unknown. In 2007 the United Nations estimated the population to be 27.1 million, while in 2008 the US Central Intelligence Agency put this figure at 32.7 million.

Almost everyone in Afghanistan is a Muslim: 84 per cent are from the majority Sunni branch of Islam, 15 per cent from the minority Shi'a branch. Afghans are devoutly religious, although differences between Sunni and Shi'a Muslims have sometimes resulted in violence.

Afghanistan is a landlocked country in central Asia.

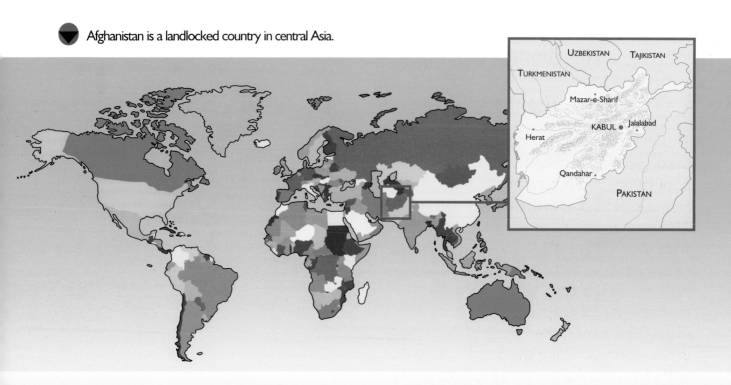

AFGHANISTAN

Simon Adams

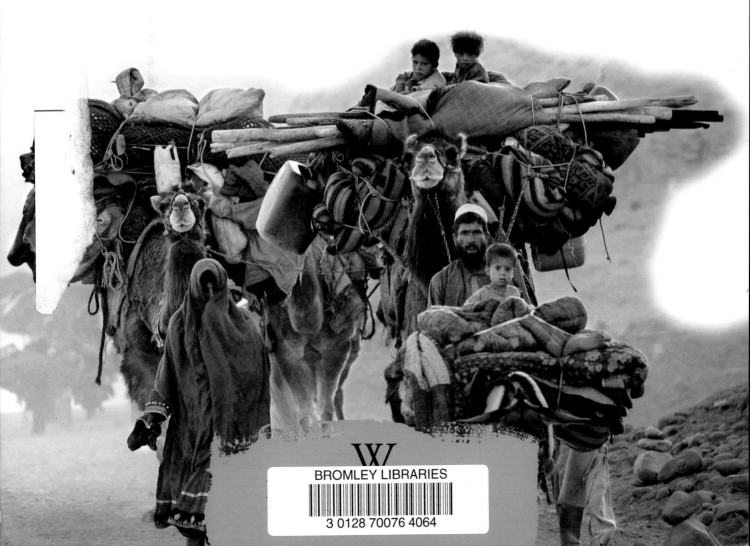

This edition 2009

Copyright © 2006, 2009 Franklin Watts

First published in 2006
by Franklin Watts
338 Euston Road
London NW1 3BH

Franklin Watts Australia
Level 17/207 Kent Street
Sydney NSW 2000

A CIP catalogue record for this book is available from the British Library.

Dewey classification number: 915.81

ISBN 978 0 7496 8927 8

Printed in Malaysia

Franklin Watts is a division of Hachette Children's Books,
an Hachette UK company
www.hachette.co.uk

Designer Rita Storey
Editor Sarah Ridley
Art Director Jonathan Hair
Editor-in-Chief John C. Miles
Picture research Diana Morris

Picture credits

David Bathgate/Corbis: 8. Bettmann/Corbis: 11.
Sergei Chirikov/epa/Corbis: 16. Eye Ubiquitous/Rex Features: 5.
Hulton-Deutsch Collection/Corbis: 7. Peter Jouvenal/Rex Features: 13.
Christiano Laruffa/Rex Features: front cover tl.
Jeroen Oerlemans/Panos: front cover b.
Reuters/Corbis: 14, 19, 20, 23, 26, 27. Reza; Webistan/Corbis: 9.
Jeffrey L. Rotman/Corbis: 24. Syed Jan Sabawoon/epa/Corbis: 1, 10.
Sipa Press/Rex Features: front cover tr,12,17,18, 21, 22.
Akhtar Soomroa/Rex Features: 15. Topfoto: 6.
Chris Young/PYMCA: 25.

*Every attempt has been made to clear copyright. Should there be any
inadvertent omission please apply to the publisher for rectification.*

▲ The Hindu Kush mountain range.

Many different peoples speaking many different languages live in Afghanistan. The Pashtuns are the largest ethnic group, making up 42 per cent of the total population, and live mainly in the south and east. The Tajiks of northeast Afghanistan are the second biggest group, with 27 per cent, followed by the Hazaras (9 per cent) and Uzbeks (9 per cent), who live in the central highlands and northern plains respectively. Turkmen (3 per cent) and other peoples live mainly in the north or along the southern border with Pakistan. All groups speak their own languages and dialects.

KNOW YOUR FACTS

The geography of Afghanistan makes it a harsh place to live. About three-quarters of the country is mountainous terrain cut with steep valleys. Flat plains lie in the north and across the south and west of the country. Three main rivers drain the country – the Amu Darya along its northern border, the Kabul in the east and the Helmand in the south. Because of its landscape and climate, only one-tenth of the land can be used for farming. Drought is a frequent problem. Despite this, about 80 per cent of Afghans rely on farming for their livelihood.

AFGHANISTAN LIES AT THE *crossroads of central and southern Asia. Its northern plains stretch into central Asia, its western and southern plains lead into Iran and Pakistan and south to the Indian Ocean, while the Hindu Kush forms the western extension of the Himalayas.*

As a result, generations of conquerors have occupied or passed through the country on their way to somewhere else (usually India), from Cyrus the Great and his Persian army in the 530s BCE, and Alexander the Great in 330 BCE, to the Mongol warlord Genghis Khan in 1220 CE.

DIVIDED TERRITORY

Few of these invaders left much mark on the country. The country therefore remained divided between its more powerful neighbours until 1747, when Ahmed Shah Durrani, a lieutenant of the Shah of Iran and a Pashtun, became king and eventually conquered a country much the same size and shape as modern-day Afghanistan.

Scottish diplomat Alexander Barnes was one of the many Britons killed during the First Afghan War in 1841.

GROUNDS FOR DEBATE

People have always asked whether Afghanistan should exist as a separate country at all. In culture, ethnic make-up and language, the northern Tajiks, Turkmen and Uzbeks look north to the largely Turkic-speaking nations of central Asia, while the Hazaras in the centre look west to Farsi-speaking Iran and the Pashtuns, Baluchs and others in the east and south look east towards Pashto- and Baluch-speaking Pakistan. Each group often has more in common with their neighbours across the border than with their fellow Afghans in the same country.

▲ King Amanullah, first king of modern-day Afghanistan.

THE GREAT GAME

In the 19th century, Afghanistan found itself caught up in the battle between the Russian and British empires – the "Great Game" – for control of central Asia and India. Twice – in 1839-42 and again in 1878-81 – the British invaded Afghanistan from India but failed to subdue the country. Meanwhile, the Russian Empire was expanding steadily southward. Both empires wanted to control Afghanistan, but in the end they decided to keep it as an independent buffer state squashed between them. In 1895 the two agreed Afghanistan's final frontiers, establishing a thin finger of land – the Wakhan Corridor, in places no more than 16 km (10 miles) wide – that stretches east to China to keep their two rival empires apart.

INDEPENDENCE

Despite this agreement, the British continued to dominate Afghan affairs until 1919, when a third war between the two countries broke out. Neither side wanted a long fight, but the Great Game had ended since Russia was now weakened by its Communist revolution of 1917 and posed no threat to the British in India. In August 1919 the British recognised Afghanistan as an independent state and agreed to leave it alone. The new king, Amanullah, began to turn Afghanistan into a modern 20th-century nation.

3 THE PASHTUNS

THE PASHTUNS ARE THE LARGEST ETHNIC GROUP *in Afghanistan, numbering as many as 13.7 million people, or 42 per cent of the total population. They live mainly in farming villages and small towns in the south and east, although there is a substantial population in the northwest. At least 200,000 Pashtuns are nomads who move around with their flocks in search of pasture and water.*

The Pashtuns are mainly Sunni Muslims and speak Pashto, one of the two official languages of Afghanistan. However, there are large numbers of Dari-speaking Pashtuns in Herat and other western parts of the country. Twelve million Pashtuns live across the border in Pakistan, and are known as Pathans.

FAMILY LIFE

Most Pashtuns are farmers, rearing and tending animals, growing fruit and other crops, and making basic agricultural tools. The heart of Pashtun society and economy is the *kalay* or village. An average-sized kalay will contain up to 200 people. All are members of several extended families descended from a common ancestor. They all attend the same mosque and share agricultural tools and household items, as well as helping each other out at harvest time or when work has to be done in the village.

Pashtuns follow the teachings of Islam but are also governed by *trabgani*, the code of behaviour that sets out how members of the kalay will co-operate and compete with each other. Pashtun behaviour in national society is governed by *Pashtunwalli*, a centuries-old code of behaviour that stresses loyalty to one's family and vengeance against injury or insult to a family member. Hospitality, bravery and individual integrity are all considered to be very important personal strengths.

 A Pashtun villager in traditional dress.

PASHTUN POWER

As the biggest group in Afghanistan, Pashtuns have traditionally run the country. Every ruler of Afghanistan from Ahmed Shah Durrani in 1747 to President Daoud, who was overthrown in 1978, has been a Pashtun. As a result, Pashtuns resent non-Pashtuns leading the country and were among the main leaders of the fight against the Soviet invaders after 1979 (see pages 12-13). Other ethnic groups, however, resent Pashtun dominance and have often rebelled or fought against them, causing great instability within the country.

A Pashtun boy in his homeland.

KNOW YOUR FACTS

In 1893 the British government in India drew the eastern border of Afghanistan along the Durand Line.
It ran straight through traditional Pashtun territories, cutting off Pashtuns in Afghanistan from Pathans in what is now the North-West Frontier Province of Pakistan. Afghan governments have never recognised the Durand Line and some people wish to reunite all Pashtuns within a new country named Pashtunistan.

LIVING ALONGSIDE PASHTUNS ARE MANY OTHER GROUPS OF PEOPLE. *The main four are the Tajiks, Hazaras, Uzbeks and Turkmen, but the country also includes groups of Aimaqs, Baluchs, Brahui, Nuristani, Pashai, Kirghiz, Qizibashes, Mongols, Arabs, Gujars, Kohistanis, Kuchis, Wakhis and Jats. There are also numbers of Hindus, Sikhs and Jews.*

TAJIKS

The Tajiks number up to 8.8 million people, or 27 per cent of the population. They live mainly in the northeast, along the border with Tajikistan, where another 6 million Tajiks live. The Tajiks are mostly Sunni Muslim, and speak Dari. The Tajiks work mainly as farmers in the fertile mountainous valleys of the region. Like the Pashtuns, they live in extended families in a *deh* or village, and follow a code of community behaviour known as *abdurzadagi*, which guides their daily lives.

HAZARAS

The 2.9 million Hazaras (9 per cent of the population) live mainly in the central mountainous region known as Hazarjarat. They speak Hazaragi, a dialect of Dari, and are mainly Shi'a Muslims. The Hazaras have Mongoloid features: the word *hazar* translates as "one thousand" in Persian and it is widely believed that the Mongol conqueror Genghis Khan left behind 1,000 troops in Afghanistan to defend the country after he attacked it in 1220. The Hazaras claim descent from these troops.

A traditional Kuchi nomadic family – with its camels and possessions – on the road to Kabul.

A traditional dome-shaped Turkmen tent with a felt roof and cane walls decorated with woven carpets.

UZBEKS AND TURKMEN

The 2.9 million Uzbeks (9 per cent of the population) live in the northern plains. They are Sunni Muslims and speak Uzbeki, the language of the 23 million Uzbeks to their north in Uzbekistan. Their land is some of the most fertile in the country, so most Uzbeks are farmers or herders, growing cotton, rice and other crops, and producing high-quality karakul lamb fleeces and hand-woven rugs. The 900,000 Turkmen (3 per cent of the population) live in the north of the country along the border with Turkmenistan, home to some 3.5 million more Turkmen. They are Sunni Muslims and speak Turkmeni, a language closely related to Uzbeki. The Turkmen are a semi-nomadic people who mix herding with settled farming, raising karakul lambs and weaving carpets.

KNOW YOUR FACTS

Differences between the various peoples in Afghanistan are very marked, as each ethnic or tribal group has its own distinct culture and language or dialect and often looks different and dresses in a different way. However generations of Afghans have come to seek work, education or refuge in the towns. Shared social and religious activities and inter-marriage have led, in the towns at least, to a new identity such as Kabuli in Kabul and Herati in Herat. Many people now consider themselves as Afghans first, and then as Tajiks, Pashtuns or whoever, second.

THE KINGS WHO RULED AFGHANISTAN *after independence from Britain in 1919 – Amanullah (1919-29), Nadir Khan (1929-33) and Zahir Shah (1933-73) – tried to modernise the country but faced constant opposition from Islamic clerics and others who did not want the traditional ways of life to change. However, the main problem for the government was its neighbour, Pakistan.*

THE PASHTUN ISSUE

When the British withdrew from India in 1947, they created the modern state of Pakistan. Afghanistan immediately raised the issue of the Durand Line, the 1893 border between Afghanistan and Pakistan that split Pashtun lands between the two countries (see page 9). Afghanistan called for the Pashtuns in Pakistan to be given the right to decide if they wanted to set up an independent Pashtun state,

WHAT DO YOU THINK?

The USSR intervened in Afghanistan after Prime Minister Nur Mohammed Taraki was overthrown in September 1979 by his revolutionary deputy, Hafizullah Amin, and the country descended into chaos. The USSR did not want communism to fail in Afghanistan, nor risk a civil war on its borders. But was it right to intervene or to try to impose communism on a traditional Islamic state? The Communist Party had fewer than 7,000 members in Afghanistan, while most Afghans saw communism as anti-Islamic.

Soviet troops on tanks moved from village to village during the 1980s.

which Afghanistan hoped to take over at some point. Pakistan refused, and gained support from the USA. Afghanistan turned to the other superpower, the communist USSR, for support.

THE SOVIETS ARRIVE

The Soviets built new roads and irrigation projects and began to train the army. In 1964 King Zahir Shah introduced major reforms, setting up an elected parliament and allowing the formation of political parties. But when these reforms began to fail, the former prime minister, Mohammed Daoud, overthrew the king in 1973 and declared a republic. Daoud tried to move the country away from the USSR but the pro-Soviet army resisted and in 1978 overthrew him, setting up a communist government.

This new government rapidly introduced revolutionary reforms, seizing land to give to peasant farmers. Many Afghans considered these changes un-Islamic and revolts quickly erupted against the government. In March 1979 a major uprising broke out in Herat. Many Soviets and Afghan communists were killed before the government restored order, leaving around 20,000 Heratis dead.

The USSR was alarmed at these events, and decided to intervene when the new prime minister was soon overthrown by his even more revolutionary deputy. It engineered a coup to overthrow the new prime minister and install a moderate

Mujahidin fighters took up arms against the occupying Soviet troops, often inflicting great losses.

successor, who then invited Soviet troops to keep order. On 27 December 1979, 80,000 Soviet troops entered the country, plunging Afghanistan into years of war.

KNOW YOUR FACTS

The USSR occupied Afghanistan from 1979 to 1989, but its troops met with fierce opposition from mujahidin guerrillas increasingly supported by the USA. As the conflict grew, 3.5 million Afghans fled to Pakistan and 1.5 million to Iran to escape the fighting. The Soviets controlled only the cities but terrorised the countryside with aircraft and heavy artillery. By the late-1980s it was clear that they could not win the war, and in 1989 they withdrew, leaving a weak communist government in charge.

AFTER THE SOVIET ARMY WITHDREW IN 1989, *the communist government of President Najibullah managed to keep control for three more years. However the mujahidin grew in strength and in April 1992 they entered Kabul and set up a new government. The mujahidin soon began to fight each other for control of Kabul, leading to at least 50,000 deaths. Then the fighting spread across the country.*

THE RISE OF THE TALIBAN

Faced with this chaos in Afghanistan, Pakistan began to support a new Islamic group called the Taliban ("seekers" of religious knowledge, or "students") in the hope of stabilising the country.

The Taliban were Islamic fundamentalists who wanted to return to the original teachings of the Qur'an, the Islamic holy book. Most of them were Pashtuns who had spent their lives in exile in Pakistan, where they studied the Qur'an in single-sex *madrassas* (Islamic schools). They therefore had little knowledge of their own country and its traditions, and not much more idea about the wider, more tolerant teachings of Islam. However, many Afghans welcomed the Taliban as they brought peace and stability.

Led by Mullah Mohammed Omar, a cleric from Qandahar, the Taliban swept through the country in 1994-95, eventually capturing Kabul in September 1996. The only parts of the country they did not control were the Panjshir Valley and the northeast, which remained under the control of the Northern Alliance, a mujahidin group of Tajiks, Uzbeks, Hazaras and others.

In 2001, the Taliban destroyed two ancient stone statues of Buddha (one shown here), as they considered them to be anti-Islamic.

TALIBAN RULE

The Taliban "Department for the Promotion of Virtue and the Prevention of Vice" imposed a strict rule on Afghanistan, based on a literal reading of the Qur'an. Girls were prevented from going to school or university or obtaining work outside the home, and all women had to cover their entire body, including their ankles, in public by wearing a *burqa*. Men were forbidden to shave or cut their beards but could not grow their hair long. Music and dancing were outlawed, and it was illegal to watch television, gamble, fly or sell kites, keep pigeons or other pet birds or shop during prayer time.

▼ Taliban members take part in an anti-American demonstration in Kabul.

Punishments for any infringements of these rules were harsh. Those guilty of minor offences were beaten with whips or imprisoned, while thieves had their hands amputated. Murderers were executed, adulterers stoned to death and homosexuals buried alive.

GROUNDS FOR DEBATE

The Taliban considered the Qur'an to be the word of God and demanded that it should be read literally and obeyed in every respect. But the Qur'an was written down 1,400 years ago, and many Muslims believe that it should be open to some more recent interpretation. The same is true of the Christian Bible, with some Christians believing that it should be understood and obeyed literally while others seek to interpret it for the present day. Should a holy book be taken as the absolute truth, or understood according to later wisdom?

THE END OF TALIBAN RULE

ALTHOUGH MANY AFGHANS SUPPORTED THE TALIBAN *because they brought peace to much of the country after years of war, others opposed them. The Taliban's strict enforcement of Islam upset moderate Muslims, while their persecution of the Shi'a and others made them many enemies.*

Since most Taliban members were Pashtun, they were disliked by non-Pashtuns. Above all, the Taliban's failure to help those left hungry and homeless after a massive earthquake in northeast Afghanistan in 1998 angered many Afghans, as it showed that the Taliban were more concerned with religious control than good government.

AL-QAEDA

The issue that brought Taliban rule to an end was their support for extreme Islamic organisations. Under the Taliban, Afghanistan became home to a large number of foreign-born Muslims who wanted to wage a *jihad* (holy war) against the enemies of Islam in order to create a pure Islamic state in the world. These enemies included not just the USA and other western countries but also the Arab governments of Saudi Arabia – where the Muslim holy cities of Mecca and Medina are – and elsewhere.

The most important group to settle in Afghanistan was al-Qaeda, set up by Osama Bin Laden. Al-Qaeda established training camps in the east of the country and attracted volunteers from Pakistan, the Arab world, Britain and the rest of Europe. From these camps, militants set out to attack the USA and other targets. In 1998 al-Qaeda launched attacks against US embassies in East Africa. The US government retaliated by attacking al-Qaeda training camps in Afghanistan. The United Nations later imposed sanctions on Afghanistan to force it to end its support for Bin Laden.

 US warplanes attack al-Qaeda training camps in Afghanistan, 1998.

Crowds cheer Northern Alliance troops as they enter Kabul in November 2001.

9/11

On 11 September 2001 al-Qaeda launched four airborne suicide attacks against the World Trade Center in New York and the Pentagon (US defence headquarters) in Washington. In response, the USA demanded that the Taliban close down all training camps and give up Bin Laden and leading al-Qaeda members for trial. When the Taliban refused, American and British troops linked up with the Northern Alliance of anti-Taliban mujahidin groups and invaded Afghanistan. Taliban rule came to an end with the fall of Kandahar in December 2001.

KNOW YOUR FACTS

Osama Bin Laden was born in 1957 into a rich merchant family in Saudi Arabia. During the mid-1980s he moved to Afghanistan to help fight the Soviet army. After the Soviets withdrew, he became fed up with infighting inside the mujahidin government and moved to Sudan, where he organised attacks against US and Arab targets. In 1994 he was invited back to Afghanistan, where he received protection in return for helping the Taliban to win control of the country. Since the overthrow of the Taliban government in 2001, his whereabouts is unknown, although some people believe that he was killed during the fighting.

8 REBUILDING AFGHANISTAN

▲ Kabul in ruins.

AFGHANISTAN HAS SUFFERED ALMOST CONSTANT *civil war and turmoil since 1978. By the time the Taliban were expelled in 2001, the country was in a terrible state.*

DEATH AND DESTRUCTION

At least one million Afghans had died during the fighting, while up to four million more were refugees in Pakistan and Iran, some of them children born in the refugee camps. At least one million more were internal refugees, displaced from their homes by the fighting, drought or the after-effects of the 1998 earthquake. Most of the roads, bridges and airfields had been destroyed, as had irrigation and water systems to feed animals and crops.

The social services of the country had collapsed completely. Almost all medical staff had left the country, and few hospitals were still open. Most schools were wrecked, and only 15 per cent of children went to primary school – all boys, as girls were denied education under the Taliban. Hunger and poverty were widespread.

A NEW START

With the fall of the Taliban, the entire government of the country collapsed. Power lay with tribal warlords, many of whom had their own private armies. The country was awash with weapons left over from the various occupying and invading armies and resistance forces.

Women members of the Loya Jirga discuss the future of their country, the first time ever that they had been involved in Afghan politics.

The US-led coalition that attacked and invaded the country in autumn 2001 took immediate steps to improve the situation. The various anti-Taliban groups met in Bonn, Germany and agreed terms for an interim government to run the country until democratic elections could be held. Thousands of international troops arrived to keep the peace, disarm the Taliban and others holding weapons, and begin reconstruction work.

In December 2001 a new 30-member interim government led by Hamid Karzai, a moderate Pashtun, took power and began to draft a new constitution. This was then presented to the Loya Jirga, a "Grand Tribal Council" of all leading

WHAT DO YOU THINK?

The new constitution of Afghanistan is intended to be as democratic as possible. It sets up a moderate Islamic state with a directly elected president and parliament. Yet Afghanistan has only ever been a democracy for nine years – from 1964 to 1973 – and few Afghans know how democratic government should work in practice. Is this new government the right one for Afghanistan, or should it have a system better suited to its Islamic, multi-ethnic history?

Afghans. After much debate, the constitution was agreed in January 2004. An electoral register of all Afghans aged 18 and over – 12.4 million men and women – who were eligible to vote was drawn up and presidential elections held in October. Eighteen candidates, including one woman, stood for election, which was won by Karzai.

EVERYDAY LIFE IS STILL VERY DIFFICULT AND DANGEROUS *for ordinary people. Large areas of Afghanistan are still littered with landmines and unexploded bombs and rockets – more than 200,000 Afghans have been killed or wounded by mines since 1979, with another 300 added to that total each month. The country contains thousands of leftover guns, so the murder rate is high and rural journeys are often vulnerable to armed robbers.*

SECURITY

The biggest problem facing Afghanistan is the continuing existence of the Taliban and al-Qaeda. Although the Taliban was defeated in 2001, its troops did not surrender their weapons. And although the US heavily bombed suspected al-Qaeda positions, its leaders disappeared into the mountains bordering Pakistan. The two groups have continued to fight both the new government and the international forces (including US, British, German and French troops) stationed in the country.

Since 2006, the Taliban has been growing again in power and support. Attacks on government and foreign soldiers have become bolder and more frequent, and the government's control is limited to the cities. In the countryside the Taliban have regained much of their former power, providing an alternative to government administration and justice – for example dealing with bandits and land disputes in Taliban courts. Many people think the Taliban could ultimately return to full power in Afghanistan.

DAILY LIFE

Since 2001, most international aid has gone to the capital, Kabul. Houses and shops have been repaired, power and water restored and some new jobs created. Most Afghans, however, live in the countryside and here the situation is critical. Years of drought, damage to irrigation channels and wells, and numerous landmines mean that most people can grow

 Workers repairing bomb-damaged roads in Kabul.

barely enough food to feed themselves, with nothing left over to sell or exchange for other goods.

The health of the average Afghan has improved slightly in recent years. The UN launched a programme to chlorinate wells and water supplies after an outbreak of cholera in Kabul. It also vaccinated millions of children against measles and polio. New health centres are being built, and doctors and nurses trained, yet 70 per cent of the population still has no access to any form of healthcare. As a result, an Afghan child today has an average life expectancy of 44 years, against 77 years for a British child.

KNOW YOUR FACTS

The resurgence of the Taliban since 2006 can be explained by several factors. These include people's anger at government corruption when officials benefit from the illegal opium trade or take a cut of foreign aid. People are also angry at the presence of foreign troops, the deaths of civilians caught up in the conflict and the lack of improvement in their lives. Ironically, the freedom of speech that is guaranteed under Afghanistan's new constitution and allows people to spread the Taliban's message is something that would quickly go if the Taliban returned to power.

Television broadcasts have now begun again after they were banned by the Taliban, and old sets are being repaired for use.

10 WOMEN AND CHILDREN

AFTER THE FALL OF THE TALIBAN, *the women of Afghanistan began to look forward to a better life. The Bonn Agreement of December 2001, setting up the interim government, agreed that women would play a part in the Loya Jirga and created a Ministry of Women's Affairs. Women got the vote and can now attend school and university and work outside the home. On paper, women are now equal but, in practice, this is far from the case.*

UNEQUAL WOMEN

Although women now enjoy considerable freedom in Kabul, the same is not true elsewhere. In the western city of Herat, the regional governor Ismail Khan –

a mujahidin warlord – has imposed Islamic laws similar to those of the Taliban and harassed and arrested women who break these laws. Women are prevented from speaking to journalists or foreign aid workers to complain about their persecution. If they are caught outside their home with a man unrelated to them, they are taken to hospital and subjected to an intimate physical examination.

Elsewhere, women are threatened with abuse and violence if they leave the home, preventing them from participating in public life. Many women still suffer rape and violence within their marriages,

Many Afghan women still wear the burqa, even though it is no longer compulsory, as they like the security and respect it can give them.

KNOW YOUR FACTS

One of the riskiest things a woman can do in Afghanistan is to give birth. Women traditionally have large families in Afghanistan: seven to ten children are not uncommon. Yet basic healthcare is so rare that 16 out of every 1,000 women die from complications during pregnancy, a figure that rises to 65 in the remote northeastern Badakhshan province. For every 1,000 children born, 165 die at birth; in Britain that figure is 5.

Thousands of children have been crippled by landmines or unexploded bombs.

but the courts are too weak to protect them. And for many women, life is as hard as ever: at least two million women were widowed during the war, leaving them to bring up their families with little or no money or support.

CHILDREN

The children of Afghanistan have suffered most from the years of turmoil. The facts about childhood today in Afghanistan make grim reading: at least 300,000 children were killed during the conflict, while 500,000 lost at least one parent and landmines crippled thousands more. Most children were denied education and good

healthcare. One in four children still die before their fifth birthday and half of all children under five are stunted due to chronic malnutrition. Although 4.6 million children now attend school, boys outnumber girls two to one, as many girls are still prevented by their religious parents from going to school.

When children reach 15 – an age when they are considered adults – the boys will be expected to earn a living to look after their families, while most girls will be married to a man chosen by their parents. Half the boys aged 15 will be able to read and write, but only one-fifth of girls.

AFGHAN FARMERS NOW GROW A CROP THAT MAKES UP *almost nine-tenths of the world's entire production of that crop, and half the annual income of the country. The crop is beautiful to look at, but deadly in its impact, for this is the opium poppy, and its product is the drug heroin.*

SUPPLYING THE WORLD

Poppy cultivation began in Afghanistan in the 1970s, after production was banned in Iran, Pakistan and Turkey. From producing about 200 tonnes or one-fifth of the world's production in 1978, Afghanistan's share rose dramatically until in 1999, under the Taliban, it reached 4,565 tonnes or almost four-fifths of the world's total production.

WHAT DO YOU THINK?

Afghanistan's opium industry is closely bound up with the war between government and international forces and the Taliban, who benefit from agricultural taxes in the rural areas they control. In 2008, the US argued for the aerial spraying of poppy fields with weedkillers. The British government disagreed, saying that aerial spraying would be seen as an attack on the livelihoods of poor Afghans and increase support for the Taliban. What do you think?

 Fields of poppies might be beautiful to look at, but they are grown to produce the deadly drug heroin.

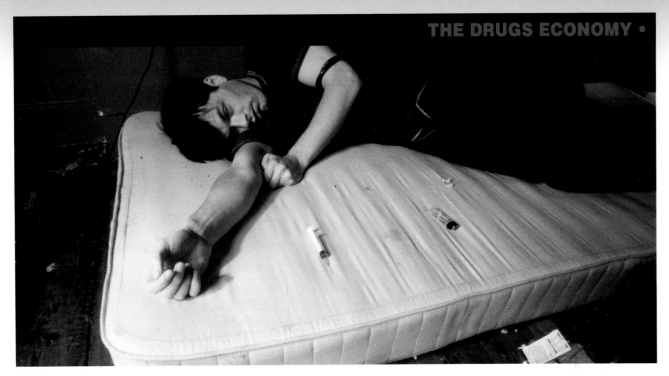

 Much of the heroin used by addicts in Europe comes from Afghan poppies.

TALIBAN BAN

In July 2000 the Taliban ordered a complete ban on poppy cultivation in order to win some favour from western nations critical of its hardline Islamic policies. Production collapsed to only 185 tonnes, forcing world prices for heroin up from US$30 a kilo in 2000 to US$700 in 2001. However, surplus Afghan stocks were then sold at the new high price, contributing vast amounts of money to the Taliban and its supporters.

VAST WEALTH

The fall of the Taliban in late 2001 coincided with the poppy-planting season. Although the new government continued the ban on poppy cultivation, farmers began to plant the crop again because it brought them huge wealth. An average small farmer can earn US$15,000 from poppies; the average Afghan earns less than US$200 a year. Long-term drought, high wheat prices and the promise of aid and development have meant that 18 out of the 32 Afghan provinces were declared "poppy-free" in 2008. But if aid does not come, this will not last. More than half of the opium comes from Helmand – which in recent years has seen some of the heaviest fighting between international (British) troops and the Taliban.

In the past, the poppies were harvested for their opium, which was then taken abroad to be converted into heroin. Today, more and more heroin is produced inside Afghanistan. The profits for manufacturers and dealers are so huge that they can bribe local and government officials to ignore their illegal activities. As drug production and trafficking affect every aspect of life, Afghanistan threatens to become a "narco-state", reliant on drugs for its income and run for the benefit of dealers and users.

WHAT'S THE FUTURE FOR AFGHANISTAN?

AFTER YEARS OF WARFARE AND TURMOIL, *the people of Afghanistan surely deserve some peace and prosperity. But what is the future for Afghanistan and its people, and how will it survive in the years to come?*

SECURITY

The main problem facing Afghanistan is the lack of security in the country. Taliban and al-Qaeda forces continue to attack international troops while several regional governors appointed by President Karzai run their provinces as independent states. The government, in effect, only controls the area around Kabul and relies on American, British and other foreign troops to keep the peace elsewhere.

Until the regional warlords can be persuaded to lay down their arms and an Afghan army trained to take over a national role, peace is still a long way off for much of the country. The existence of large amounts of leftover weaponry outside government control does not help the peace process.

ECONOMICS

The other big problem facing Afghanistan is its economy. The decades of fighting devastated the country, leaving industry and agriculture in ruins, and wrecking communications, roads, power lines and water supplies. The only profitable crop is the opium poppy, and that is illegal.

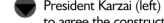 President Karzai (left) and Turkmenistan's President Niyazov (in red tie) at a signing ceremony in 2002 to agree the construction of a gas pipeline between their countries.

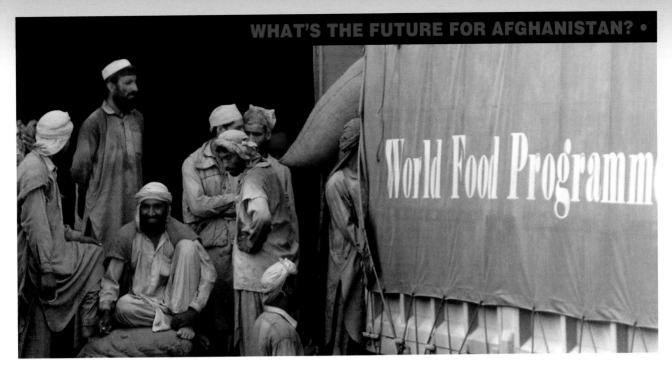

Afghans unload a delivery of food aid. Afghanistan needs the support of the world if it is to rebuild.

However, the country has supplies of natural gas and coal, while its rivers can be dammed to provide hydroelectric power. Afghanistan also lies on the direct route for a pipeline carrying natural gas from Turkmenistan south to Pakistan, which when built will generate millions of dollars' income each year. Traditional strengths, such as wool production and carpet weaving, will help also.

DEMOCRACY

Democracy survived for only nine years in Afghanistan before it was ended in 1973 and only began again in 2004. For people brought up in a largely tribal society where you obey your tribal leaders and elders, the idea of democratic government where everyone is equal and can have their say is very foreign. Trying to establish a national government where all the different ethnic groups are involved and feel they are being consulted will be difficult. If it works, Afghanistan will be able to overcome its many internal differences and begin to work together as one country. If it fails, the country could slide back into civil war or Taliban control.

MISTAKES LEARNT?

In an interview in 2008, President Karzai said that two of the biggest setbacks in Afghanistan since the fall of the Taliban in 2001 had been the failure to hunt down the Taliban and al-Qaeda in their training camps (many of which are in neighbouring Pakistan) and to educate and equip Afghans with new skills. More optimistically, in December 2008 President Karzai and Pakistan's President Ali Zardari agreed a joint approach to fighting Taliban and al-Qaeda forces in the Afghanistan-Pakistan border region. Co-operation with its neighbours holds one of the keys to Afghanistan's future.

530s BCE: Cyrus the Great makes Afghanistan part of the Persian Empire.

330 BCE: Alexander the Great conquers Afghanistan.

50 CE: Afghanistan becomes part of the central Asian Kushan Empire.

250: The country becomes part of the Persian Sasanian Empire.

652: Arab armies invade, bringing Islam.

822: Arab or Persian dynasties begin to rule.

1220: Genghis Khan devastates the north and west of Afghanistan.

1369: Timur invades and makes the country part of his Timurid Empire.

1510: The Timurid Empire collapses; Babur, a descendant of Timur, conquers the country and invades India, creating the Mughal Empire.

1530: On the death of Babur, Afghanistan is divided between an Uzbek north, Mughal east and Persian west.

1749: Ahmed Shah Durrani, a Pashtun leader, is elected king and creates an independent Afghanistan.

1839–42: First Afghan War against the British.

1873: The British and Russians agree the northern Afghan border.

1878–81: Second Afghan War against the British.

1884: The Russians complete their conquest of central Asia.

1893: The British fix the Afghan-Indian border along the Durand Line, splitting Pashtun lands in two.

1895: Russia and Britain create the "Afghan Finger" or Wakhan Corridor to keep their two empires apart.

1901: Habibullah becomes king.

1919: Feb: Habibullah is assassinated; his son Amanullah becomes king.

May: Third Afghan War against the British.

June: The war ends after the British bomb Kabul and Jalalabad.

Aug: The British recognise Afghan independence.

1928: Amanullah proposes major reforms; revolution breaks out against him.

1929: Jan: Amanullah abdicates; an illiterate Tajik warlord, Bacha Saqao, seizes the throne.

July: General Nadir Khan becomes king.

1932: The first university is founded in Kabul.

1933: Nadir Khan is assassinated; his son, Zahir Shah, becomes king.

1946: Afghanistan joins the United Nations.

1947: The British withdraw from India; Afghanistan raises the issue of the Durand Line with Pakistan and asks the USSR for support.

1956: The first Five-Year Plan to modernise the country is introduced with Soviet aid.

1964: King Zahir Shah introduces democratic reforms, becoming a constitutional monarch.

1973: Mohammed Daoud overthrows the king and declares a republic.

1978: The army overthrows Daoud and sets up a pro-Soviet communist state under Nur Mohammed Taraki.

1979: March: an anti-government uprising occurs in Herat.

Sept: Taraki is murdered by his deputy, Hafizullah Amin.

Dec: A Soviet-backed coup overthrows Amin and installs the moderate, Babrak Karmal, as president; Soviet troops are "invited" into the country to keep order.

1980: The mujahidin fight the Soviet occupation; refugees flee into Pakistan and Iran.

1982: The USA begins to fund the mujahidin.

1986: Mohammed Najibullah becomes president.

1989: Soviet troops withdraw.

1992: The mujahidin overthrow Najibullah; civil war erupts between rival mujahidin groups.

1994: The Taliban captures Kandahar; Osama Bin Laden returns to the country to set up al-Qaeda bases.

1995: The Taliban captures Herat.

1996: The Taliban captures Kabul and soon rules most of the country; the Northern Alliance leads the resistance to Taliban rule.

1998: Feb: A major earthquake kills thousands in northeast Afghanistan.

Aug: The US launch missile strikes on al-Qaeda bases after the bombing of US embassies in Africa.

1999–2002: A severe drought occurs.

2000: The UN imposes sanctions on Afghanistan.

2001: March: The Taliban destroys giant statues of the Buddha at Bamiyan.

Sept: 9/11 attacks on New York and Washington by al-Qaeda.

Oct: The US begins to attack Afghanistan.

Dec: Anti-Taliban groups sign the Bonn Agreement, setting up an interim government.

Dec: The Taliban government falls after the capture of Kandahar. Hamid Karzai is declared the president of an interim government.

2002: June: Loya Jirga meets and confirms Karzai as the interim president.

2004: Jan: Loya Jirga agrees a new constitution.

Sept: An electoral register is drawn up.

Oct: A presidential election is held and won by Hamid Karzai.

2005: Sept: Parliamentary elections held.

2006: Jan: International conference in London, dubbed "Bonn Two" after the December 2001 meeting, agrees substantial financial and military aid for Afghanistan.

2007: August The United Nations reports that opium production has reached record levels.

2008: June The Taliban organises a jail-break from Kandahar prison, freeing at least 350 of its members.

2008: December: President Karzai and Pakistan's President Ali Zardari agree a joint approach to fighting Taliban and al-Qaeda forces in the Afghanistan-Pakistan border region.

BASIC FACTS

OFFICIAL NAME: Islamic Republic of Afghanistan.

POPULATION: 27.1 million up to 32.7 million.

SIZE: 652,225 sq km (251,824 sq miles).

BORDERS: China, Iran, Pakistan, Tajikistan, Turkmenistan, Uzbekistan.

CITIES: Kabul (capital), Kandahar, Herat, Mazar-e-Sharif, Jalalabad.

OFFICIAL LANGUAGES: Pashto, Dari.

RELIGION: Sunni Muslim 84 per cent, Shi'a Muslim 15 per cent, other 1 per cent.

LIFE EXPECTANCY: 44 years (both men and women) (UN figures).

ETHNIC MAKE-UP: Pashtun 42 per cent, Tajik 27 per cent, Hazara 9 per cent, Uzbek 9 per cent, Turkmen 3 per cent, other 10 per cent.

CURRENCY: New afghani.

YEAR OF INDEPENDENCE: 1919.

NATIONAL DAY: 19 August, Independence Day.

Ally A country or political group linked with another by treaty, friendship or common purpose.

Buffer state A small, usually neutral state, between two rival, powerful states.

Burqa A garment worn by women during the Taliban era that covers them from head to toe, leaving no part of their body exposed.

Coalition An alliance or union between nations, groups of people, or political parties.

Communism The belief in a society that exists without different social classes and in which everyone is equal and all property owned by the people.

Constitution A written document stating the principles on which a country is to be governed.

Dialect A form of language spoken in a particular area or by a particular group of people with some words, grammar and pronunciation different from the parent language.

Empire A group of peoples or countries governed by a single ruler or system.

Ethnic Racial, religious, linguistic, cultural and other aspects held in common by a group of people.

Extended family A family unit of parents and children as well as other blood relatives such as uncles, aunts and grandparents from three or more generations.

Fundamentalist Someone who prefers a strict interpretation of a holy book, such as the Qur'an.

Guerrilla A member of an irregular, politically motivated armed force outside the control or command of a regular army.

Interim government A temporary government running a country until a permanent government can be elected or take power.

Jihad An Islamic holy war against infidels or non-believers.

Landlocked A country entirely surrounded by land and with no coastline or access to the sea.

Loya Jirga The Grand Tribal Council of all Afghans, the highest representative organisation in Afghanistan.

Madrassa An Islamic religious school.

Minority A group of people who form a distinct but small group within a nation and who are different from the majority of the population.

Mullah A Muslim cleric or teacher.

Mujahidin Islamic fundamentalist freedom fighters.

Nomad A person who moves with his animals in search of grazing land.

Qur'an (Koran) The Islamic holy book.

Republic A country governed by an elected head of state called a president.

Shi'a The minority branch of Islam which believes the succession to the Prophet Muhammad was unfairly taken by those outside his immediate family; Shi'a means "partisans of Ali", the cousin and son-in-law of Muhammad.

Sunni The majority branch of Islam who take their name from *sunna*, meaning "true path".

Superpower A country with an overwhelming military and economic power, such as the USSR or USA.

United Nations The international organisation established in 1945 to promote peace and co-operation between countries.

USSR The Union of the Soviet Socialist Republics, or Soviet Union, which existed from 1922 to 1991; commonly known as Russia.

Warlord A tribal chieftain holding considerable power over a region of a country through his own private army.

World Health Organisation An agency of the United Nations, set up in 1948 to promote health and tackle disease around the world.

USEFUL WEBSITES
http://www.pajhwok.com/
The website of the independent Afghan news agency Pajhwok Afghan News.

http://www.afghanistans.com
Lots of easy-to-access information about the country, its people and their history.

http://www.pbs.org/newshour/indepth_coverage/asia/afghanistan/
A student-friendly website on Afghanistan and the "war on terror" from the US Public Broadcasting Service.

http://news.bbc.co.uk/1/hi/in_depth/south_asia/2004/afghanistan/default.stm
An in-depth look at the issues facing Afghanistan from the BBC News website.

Note to parents and teachers:
Every effort has been made by the Publishers to ensure that the websites in this book are suitable for children, that they are of the highest educational value, and that they contain no inappropriate or offensive material. However, because of the nature of the Internet, it is impossible to guarantee that the contents of these sites will not be altered. We strongly advise that Internet access is supervised by a responsible adult.